MILWAUKEE BREWERS

ALL-TIME GREATS

BY TED COLEMAN

Book design by Jake Slavik
Cover design by Jake Slavik

Photographs ©: Larry Radloff/Icon Sportswire/AP Images, cover (top), 1 (top); David Durochik/AP Images, cover (bottom), 1 (bottom), 6; Ed Kolenovsky/AP Images, 4; R.J. Hinkle/AP Images, 9; Jim Palmer/AP Images, 10; John Cordes/Icon Sportswire/AP Images, 12; Larry Goren/Four Seam Images/AP Images, 15; Jeffrey Phelps/AP Images, 16; Scott Boehm/AP Images, 19; Joe Robbins/Icon Sportswire/AP Images, 21

Press Box Books, an imprint of Press Room Editions.

ISBN
978-1-63494-504-2 (library bound)
978-1-63494-530-1 (paperback)
978-1-63494-580-6 (epub)
978-1-63494-556-1 (hosted ebook)

Library of Congress Control Number: 2022901754

Distributed by North Star Editions, Inc.
2297 Waters Drive
Mendota Heights, MN 55120
www.northstareditions.com

Printed in the United States of America
082022

ABOUT THE AUTHOR

Ted Coleman is a freelance sportswriter and children's book author who lives in Louisville, Kentucky, with his trusty Affenpinscher, Chloe.

TABLE OF CONTENTS

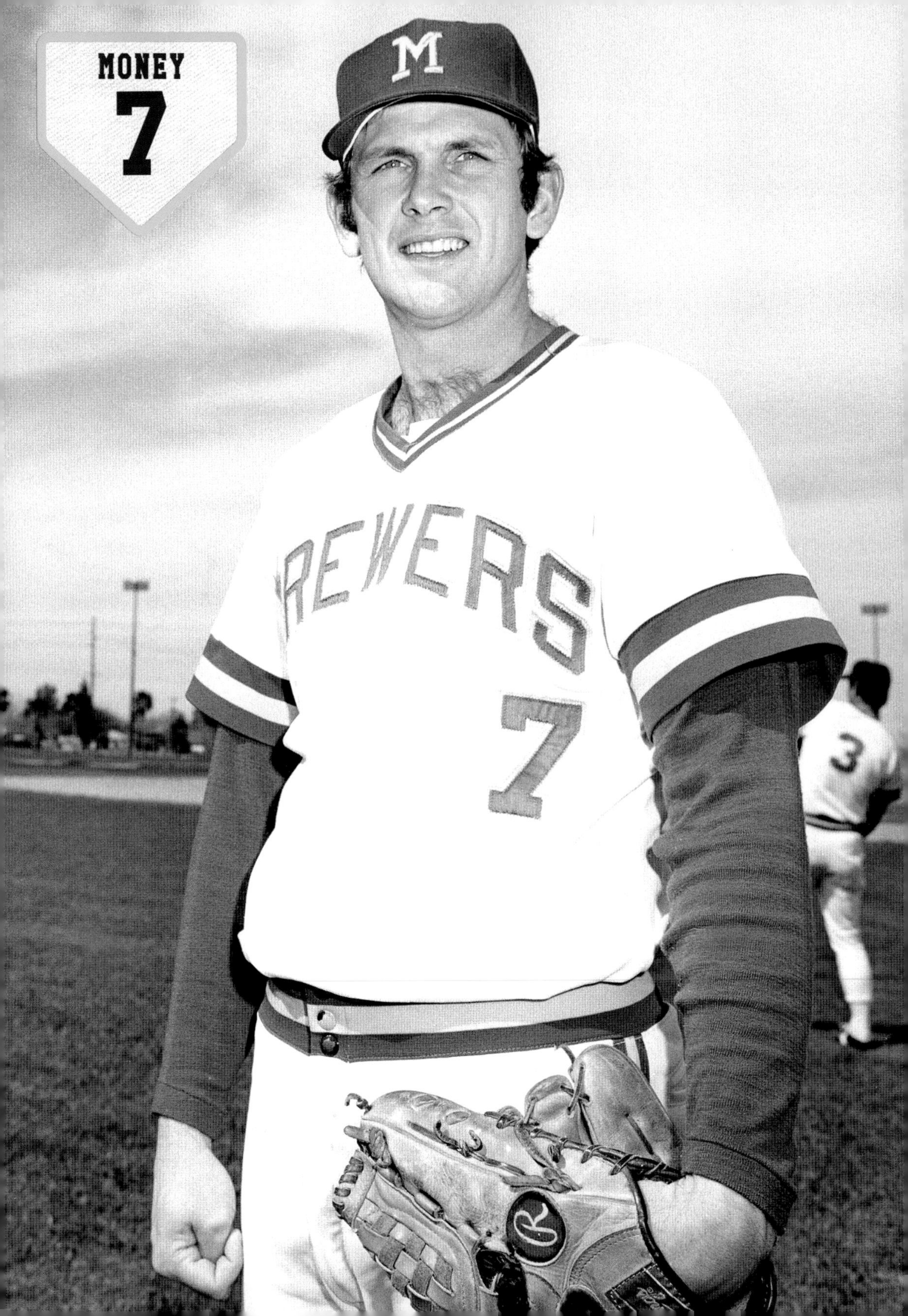
MONEY
7

CHAPTER 1

SOMETHING BREWING

The Milwaukee Brewers began playing in 1969. At the time, they were known as the Seattle Pilots. However, the Pilots lasted only a year in Seattle. In 1970, they moved to Wisconsin and became the Milwaukee Brewers.

Fans didn't have much to cheer about for the first few years. Even so, Brewers fans came to love their players. Pitcher **Jim Slaton** played on a lot of bad teams. But the right-hander ended up as the team's all-time leader in wins and innings pitched.

The Brewers recorded their first winning season in 1978. Infielder **Don Money** led

YOUNT
19

the way. Money made his fourth All-Star Game that year. The Brewers were starting to build something special.

Center fielder **Gorman Thomas** had a lousy .230 batting average as a Brewer. He didn't have speed, either. But Milwaukee fans loved him anyway. The slugger could hit balls clear out of the park.

Fans also loved **Robin Yount**. He was one of the best hitters in baseball history. Yount earned two Most Valuable Player (MVP) Awards during his 20-year career. He also recorded more than 3,000 career hits. And he did it all in a Brewers uniform.

Yount's double-play partner at second base was **Jim Gantner**. Gantner was a Wisconsin native. Like Yount, he spent his entire career with Milwaukee. Gantner was known for his determined attitude and his steady play.

STAT SPOTLIGHT

CAREER HITS
BREWERS RECORD
Robin Yount: 3,142

On the mound, **Mike Caldwell** was Milwaukee's ace. The left-hander was a fiery competitor when he pitched. In 1978, Caldwell was one of the best pitchers in baseball. He posted a 22–9 record that season.

First baseman **Cecil Cooper** could hit for both average and power. He hit .300 or better in each of his first seven seasons in Milwaukee. He also blasted 20 or more homers five times.

The final piece of the puzzle was **Paul Molitor**. Molitor played all over the field. He was also an outstanding hitter.

1982 MAGIC

In their first 50 years, the Brewers reached only one World Series. But the 1982 team was loaded with stars. Robin Yount and Paul Molitor led the way. A team not known for winning was dominant that year. And they nearly won it all. They lost to the St. Louis Cardinals in seven games.

MOLITOR
4

Molitor spent 15 years in Milwaukee. In 1982,
he and Yount led the Brew Crew to their first
World Series appearance.

FINGERS
34

CHAPTER 2
AFTER THE SERIES

Much of the World Series core stayed with the team for several more years. Star reliever **Rollie Fingers** became the team's all-time leader in saves. Fingers ended his career after the 1985 season. The Brewers later retired his number.

Slowly, the World Series memories started to fade. The Brewers couldn't keep up their winning ways. Even so, Milwaukee still had some great players. Outfielder **Ben Oglivie** stayed with the team through 1986. Oglivie earned three trips to the All-Star Game during his career.

HIGUERA
49

Teddy Higuera was one of Milwaukee's best pitchers after their World Series era. Higuera had been a star in Mexico. The Brewers called him up in 1985. He pitched his entire nine-year career in Milwaukee. And in 1986, Higuera was an All-Star.

Pitcher **Dan Plesac** ended up breaking the team's saves record. He was one of baseball's steadiest relievers of the 1980s. From 1987 to 1989, Plesac made three All-Star Games in a row.

A pair of hitters brought some excitement to Milwaukee in the late 1990s and early 2000s. By that point, the Brewers hadn't posted a winning season in a while. But fans enjoyed watching **Jeff Cirillo** and **Geoff Jenkins** play. Cirillo became the team's all-time leader

STAT SPOTLIGHT

CAREER SAVES
BREWERS RECORD
Dan Plesac: 133

in batting average. He also had a great glove at third base.

Meanwhile, Jenkins was the team's best slugger since Gorman Thomas. Jenkins cranked out 212 homers in a Brewers uniform. At the time, that was second in team history. Only Robin Yount had more.

In the 2000s, pitcher **Ben Sheets** gave Brewers fans hope. Sheets was one of the top prospects in baseball. The right-hander arrived in 2001. He was an All-Star right

HAMMERIN' HANK

The legendary **Hank Aaron** began his career with the Milwaukee Braves in 1954. He stayed with the team after it moved to Atlanta in 1966. At the end of his career, Aaron returned to Milwaukee for two years. He hit the last of his 755 career homers in a Brewers uniform. Despite Aaron's brief stint with the Brewers, the team retired his No. 44 uniform for his time in Milwaukee.

SHEETS
15

away. Sheets had excellent control over the ball. He also fooled batters with a great blend of pitches. Unfortunately, injuries shortened his career. Even so, Sheets still ranks among the team's pitching leaders in many categories.

BRAUN
8

CHAPTER 3
NEW BREW CREW

By 2007, it had been 25 years since the Brewers last reached the postseason. That was also the year **Ryan Braun** began his career. And before long, Braun helped the Brewers become winners again. Braun smashed the team record for home runs. He also posted a career batting average of .296.

STAT SPOTLIGHT

CAREER HOME RUNS
BREWERS RECORD

Ryan Braun: 352

Braun may own the team's career home run record. But slugger **Prince Fielder** set the team's single-season record. In fact, Fielder had the top two seasons in Brewers history. In 2007, he blasted 50 homers. He followed that up with 46 in 2009. Fielder would have broken the team's career record if he had stayed in Milwaukee. However, he signed with the Detroit Tigers in 2012.

The Brewers weren't all about power, though. They also boasted one of the top pitchers in baseball. Right-hander **Yovani Gallardo** recorded at least 200 strikeouts every year from 2009 to 2012. Of the 10 best strikeout seasons in Brewers history, three belong to Gallardo. In 2011, Gallardo helped Milwaukee win its first postseason series in 29 years.

FIELDER
28

In 2018, outfielder **Christian Yelich** won the batting title and hit 36 homers. Not surprisingly, he won the MVP Award. The next year, Yelich won the batting title again and hit 44 homers. Best of all, the Brewers reached the postseason in each of his first four seasons with the team.

Reliever **Josh Hader** made a name for himself as one of the league's best closers. Hader's fastball could reach speeds of 100 miles per hour. Meanwhile, **Corbin Burnes** was one of the best starting pitchers in

VOICE OF THE BREWERS

Bob Uecker was the broadcaster for the Brewers from almost the beginning. He became the voice of the Brewers in 1971. As of 2021, he was still going strong. Uecker also had a six-year playing career in the major leagues. It included two seasons with the Milwaukee Braves.

YELICH
22

baseball. In 2021, he became the first Brewer
to win the Cy Young Award since 1982.
Milwaukee fans hoped their team would soon
make another World Series run.

TIMELINE

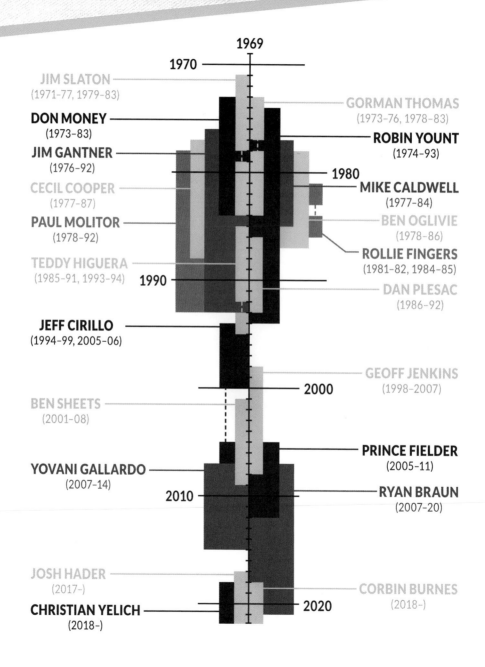

1969

1970

JIM SLATON
(1971–77, 1979–83)

GORMAN THOMAS
(1973–76, 1978–83)

DON MONEY
(1973–83)

ROBIN YOUNT
(1974–93)

JIM GANTNER
(1976–92)

1980

CECIL COOPER
(1977–87)

MIKE CALDWELL
(1977–84)

PAUL MOLITOR
(1978–92)

BEN OGLIVIE
(1978–86)

TEDDY HIGUERA
(1985–91, 1993–94)

ROLLIE FINGERS
(1981-82, 1984–85)

1990

DAN PLESAC
(1986–92)

JEFF CIRILLO
(1994–99, 2005–06)

GEOFF JENKINS
(1998–2007)

2000

BEN SHEETS
(2001–08)

PRINCE FIELDER
(2005–11)

YOVANI GALLARDO
(2007–14)

RYAN BRAUN
(2007–20)

2010

JOSH HADER
(2017–)

CORBIN BURNES
(2018–)

CHRISTIAN YELICH
(2018–)

2020

TEAM FACTS

MILWAUKEE BREWERS

Team history: Seattle Pilots (1969), Milwaukee Brewers (1970–)

World Series titles: 0*

Key managers:

Harvey Kuenn (1975, 1982–83)

   160–118–1 (.576)

Phil Garner (1992–99)

   563–617 (.477)

Craig Counsell (2015–)

   529–479 (.525)

MORE INFORMATION

To learn more about the Milwaukee Brewers, go to **pressboxbooks.com/AllAccess**.

These links are routinely monitored and updated to provide the most current information available.

*through 2021

GLOSSARY

ace
The best starting pitcher on a team.

closer
A relief pitcher who usually plays in the ninth inning to protect a lead.

double play
A play during which the fielding team records two outs.

era
A period of time in history.

postseason
A set of games to decide a league's champion.

prospect
A player that people expect to do well at a higher level.

reliever
A pitcher who does not start the game.

slugger
A batter known for hitting home runs.

INDEX